*It took a village to build this book. Special thanks to
my agent, Ronnie; critique partners Beth, Heather, and Kate;
and my wonderful friend Shannon for lending an ear!*

—M. L.

To my mom, Terri, who instilled in me a deep love of science.

—A. H.

STERLING CHILDREN'S BOOKS
New York

An Imprint of Sterling Publishing Co., Inc.
1166 Avenue of the Americas
New York, NY 10036

STERLING CHILDREN'S BOOKS and the distinctive Sterling Children's Books logo
are registered trademarks of Sterling Publishing Co., Inc.

Text © 2020 Michelle Lord
Cover and interior illustrations © 2020 Alleanna Harris

ISBN 978-1-4549-3137-9

Library of Congress Cataloging-in-Publication Data

Names: Lord, Michelle, author. | Harris, Alleanna, illustrator.
Title: Patricia's vision : the doctor who saved sight / by Michelle Lord ;
    illustrated by Alleanna Harris.
Description: New York, NY : Sterling Publishing Co., Inc., [2020] | Audience:
    Ages 5+. | Audience: K to grade 3.
Identifiers: LCCN 2019012072 | ISBN 9781454931379 (book / hc_plc with jacket
    picture book)
Subjects: LCSH: Bath, Patricia, 1942—Juvenile literature. |
    Ophthalmologists—Biography—Juvenile literature. | Women
    inventors—Biography—Juvenile literature. | African American
    women—Biography—Juvenile literature. | Eye—Surgery—Juvenile
    literature. | Lasers in surgery—History—Juvenile literature. | LCGFT:
    Biographies.
Classification: LCC RE36.B2855 L67 2020 | DDC 617.7092 [B] --dc23
LC record available at https:_lccn.loc.gov_2019012072

Distributed in Canada by Sterling Publishing Co., Inc.
c/o Canadian Manda Group, 664 Annette Street
Toronto, Ontario M6S 2C8, Canada
Distributed in the United Kingdom by GMC Distribution Services
Castle Place, 166 High Street, Lewes, East Sussex BN7 1XU, England
Distributed in Australia by NewSouth Books
University of New South Wales, Sydney, NSW 2052, Australia

For information about custom editions, special sales, and premium and corporate purchases, please contact
Sterling Special Sales at 800-805-5489 or specialsales@sterlingpublishing.com.

Manufactured in China

Lot #:
2 4 6 8 10 9 7 5 3 1
10/19

sterlingpublishing.com

The art for this book was created digitally
Cover and interior design by Irene Vandervoort

Patricia's VISION

THE DOCTOR WHO SAVED SIGHT

BY Michelle Lord

ILLUSTRATED BY Alleanna Harris

STERLING CHILDREN'S BOOKS

New York

Harlem, New York City, late 1940s.
Young Patricia Bath was curious. She peered at a man begging
for coins. Folks in her neighborhood strolled past him, but
Patricia watched and wondered . . .

Why are his eyes cloudy?
How did it happen?

She shut her eyes and pondered,
What's it like to live in the dark?

Other little girls played nurse. But six-year-old Patricia declared, "I want to be a doctor!" All the doctors Patricia knew were men. A medical degree required years and years of study and cost money Patricia's family didn't have. But she saw possibility when others couldn't.

Both of her parents stressed the importance of education and hard work. Her mother cooked and cleaned a Park Avenue apartment to save money for Patricia's education. She encouraged her daughter's interest in science by surprising her with a chemistry set. Patricia learned about the big, wide world from her father's stories of working aboard merchant ships. She knew an education would take her places!

All the while, Patricia doctored her dolls. Poking her needle into the tattered cloth and back through the other side,
she stitched,
she snipped,
and she knotted.
She mended her dolls with bandages, splints, and neat stitches and never lost sight of her dream.

Patricia grew, and so did her curiosity.

In high school, science made Patricia's pulse race.
Other teens watched TV. Patricia pressed her eyes to a
microscope, inspecting insects she caught.

Patricia loved learning. She worked hard and kept her eye on the future.

"I was always a curious child."

In college, she memorized,

she multiplied,

and she measured.

When she wasn't poring over beakers, burners, or ionic bonds, she volunteered to read to the blind. Four years passed in a blur.

In medical school, she studied everything from broken bones to kidney stones, inside and out, from head to toe. By the time she finished, she knew exactly what kind of doctor she wanted to be: an ophthalmologist, a surgeon who treats the eyes.

After four years of medical school, she slipped out of her cap and gown and into a crisp, white coat. She was now Doctor Patricia Bath!

"I decided to get the training, education, skill set so I could achieve miracles."

Dr. Bath tackled her first project in her own Harlem neighborhood. So many blind patients gathered at the Harlem Hospital Eye Clinic. Dr. Bath wondered, *Why?* She wanted excellent eye care for *everyone*. Most of these patients had never been examined by an ophthalmologist. Swallowing her sorrow, she asked her professors to help. They said yes and operated for free. Dr. Bath saw possibility when others couldn't.

"Eyesight
is a basic
human right."

Dr. Bath couldn't wait to begin her career as an ophthalmologist. She moved across the country to join the famed Jules Stein Eye Institute in California. Walking into work that first morning, she had no idea she was the first woman on the faculty! Her eyes widened upon finding her new office . . .

away from the others,
in the basement,
next to the lab animals . . .

ES

Patricia
Bath

She marched upstairs and demanded a workspace equal to what the other new professors had.

At times, she wondered why the others took the easy cases of the rich and famous. They gave Dr. Bath the difficult patients. But she straightened her lab coat and got to work.

"Taking the high road may be arduous and long, but it will lead to justice and triumph."

She was proud to care for the so-called hopelessly blind.
What if I could give my patients the gift of sight? she wondered. . . .

Other doctors said, "It's impossible." Dr. Bath said, "I choose
miracles."

TIP-TAP. TIP-TAP. A blind veteran found his way to her office. Dr. Bath decided the best treatment was to replace his damaged cornea—the covering of the eyeball—with an artificial cornea.

"I felt that being able to restore sight to the blind was really the highest call of what I could do . . ."

In the operating room,
under hot lights,
she squinted through a microscope for hours—

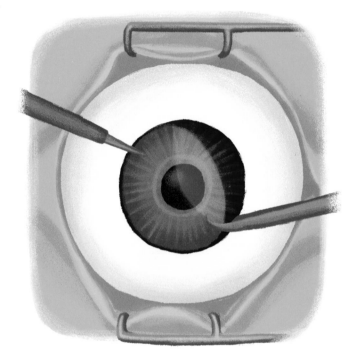

cutting away scar tissue, fitting a plastic cornea until her
fingers ached. An artificial cornea contains a tiny tube that
projects the light and returns patient's vision. Dr. Bath placed
the device through his cornea. Sewing it in place, she wove her
needle in and out as she had when she was a little girl.

When Dr. Bath p-e-e-l-e-d away the bandages, her patient's face shined like a lamp. "I can see the light!" With her help, patients read signs, marveled at colors, and walked without canes. They even drove cars!

Dr. Bath saw possibility when others couldn't.

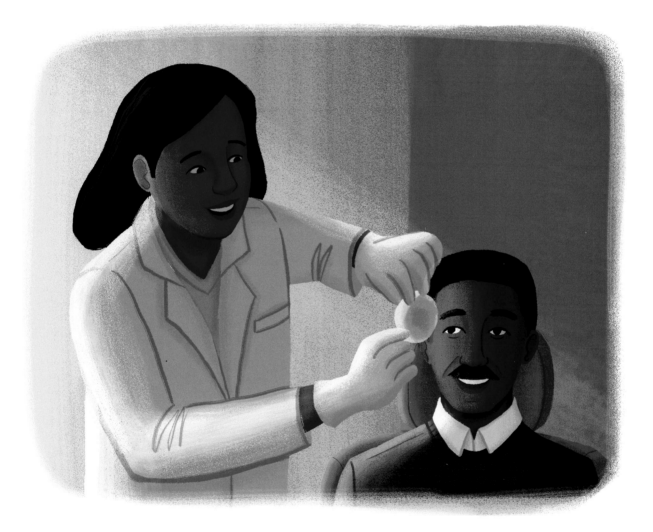

"Each time I have restored or improved someone's vision through surgery, it's a very special moment."

One day, a patient called on Dr. Bath for help. Shining a bright light into her patient's eyes, Dr. Bath discovered the problem. She shook her head. A thin layer of tissue, called a membrane, had grown in the eye after surgery. The woman could no longer see.

Dr. Bath spent many sleepless nights, tossing and turning, wondering how to help. One night, she had an idea!

A laser.
A laser makes a narrow beam of light.
So narrow that it becomes intense.
So intense that it can cut like a knife.
Other doctors used lasers on the skin, inside the body, and sometimes focused inside the eye. Never before had doctors used a laser tool that could be guided with the ease and control of a pencil. This was Dr. Bath's new idea. How could she take it from her imagination to the operating room?

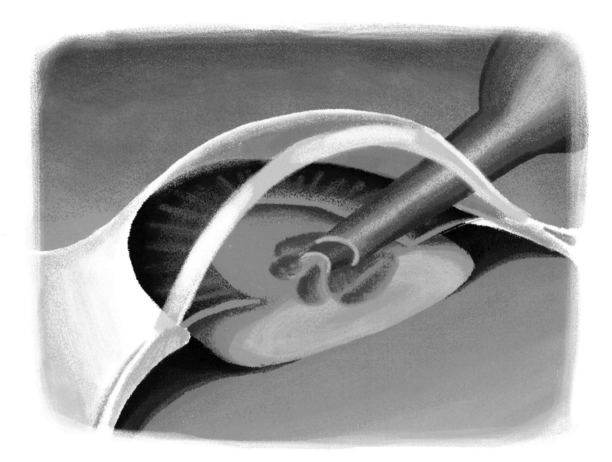

In her mind, she saw a probe that could focus a laser beam through a tiny fiber as thin as a single strand of hair. Dr. Bath remembered the man with the cloudy eyes from her childhood. Doctors already used lasers on the cornea. *Why not on a cloudy lens?* she thought. *BOOM!* She realized her laser probe design could be used to remove cataracts, a common condition where the lens of the eye turns cloudy and causes blindness.

"Unthinkable."
"Preposterous!"
"It can't be done," said the other doctors.
But she kept thinking big thoughts about the tool that didn't exist. YET.

"Remember that
the limits of science are not
the limits of your imagination."

Dr. Bath traveled to Europe in 1986 to experiment with the best lasers.

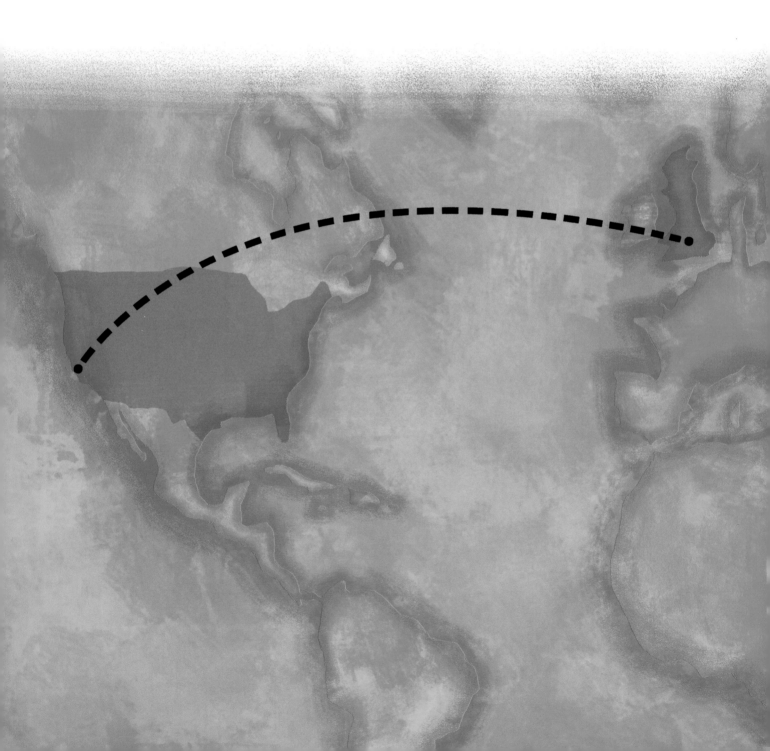

She planned, plotted, and predicted.

Finally, she gathered parts for a tool that only existed in her mind.

I.V. tubing.

Stainless steel pipe.

Optical fibers.

She wasted no time. She fitted. She fashioned. She fused.

And she refused to give up. She had to see if her idea worked.

Alone.
    Long after midnight,
    raindrops pelted the window as Dr. Bath tested different
lasers on eye tissue.
    Her mind churned. *Maybe. Possibly. This could work.*

She aimed the argon fluoride laser at the lens and fired, but the cataract was still there.

Next she fired the krypton fluoride laser. Still not enough power.

Dr. Bath leaned close. If the wavelength wasn't just right, the eyeball *might* burst.

She aimed the xenon chloride laser and fired.

POP. POP. POP.

Although she could not see the laser beam, she watched
the cataract vaporize in a few zaps.

Dr. Bath tossed her papers into the air. "EUREKA!"

Her invention worked. She called the new tool the Laserphaco Probe.

Back home, she applied for a patent, an official document to prove that she was the inventor of Laserphaco. And she waited. . . .

*"I was not seeking to be the first,
I was only attempting to do my thing."*

Months later, Dr. Bath found an envelope from the United States Patent and Trademark office in her mailbox.

Her hands trembled as she ripped open the flap.

On May 17, 1988, Dr. Bath was granted her first patent for her Laserphaco Probe.

Her eyes flooded with tears of joy!

Even in retirement, Dr. Bath never lost sight of her goal.

While climbing Mount Kilimanjaro in Tanzania, she learned about a school for the blind. When she visited, she found a mud building, a classroom without braille books, and children in need. Her heart sank. She hunted all around town but couldn't find so much as a magnifying glass to help them see. What could she do? She returned home, but wondered . . .

Do these children have a future?
What do they need?
How can I help?

Once again, Dr. Bath saw a way where others could not. *Technology.*

If the children could not read words with their eyes, they could read braille computer keyboards with their fingertips. Dr. Bath sent computers to the school in Tanzania. Now, the students could read words and calculate homework problems. Computers gave them not only books, but a world of information where their lives before had been dark. Here, too, she gave the gift of sight. She called it "Computer Vision."

"In my childhood, I developed a love and respect for humanity and wanted to help heal the sick."

"... I believe that someday
the blind will see."

Dr. Patricia Bath saw possibility wherever she went.

TIMELINE

1942 On November 4th, Mr. Bath, Mrs. Bath, and big brother welcomed Patricia Bath. She was born at home in Harlem, New York City.

1959 Teenage Patricia won a spot in a National Science Foundation summer science program, where she researched cancer cells.

1960 Her results were published in a scientific paper, and she was interviewed by the *New York Times*. She was granted *Mademoiselle* magazine's merit award for her work.

1964 Patricia graduated from Hunter College with a degree in chemistry.

1968 Patricia graduated from Howard University College of Medicine.

1968-1969 Dr. Bath interned at Harlem Hospital, where she persuaded doctors to bring eye surgery to the eye clinic, which it had never done before.

1970 She completed a fellowship in ophthalmology at Columbia University.

1973 Dr. Bath trained at New York University, where she was the first African American to complete a residency in ophthalmology.

1975 She became the first female faculty member at the UCLA School of Medicine Jules Stein Eye Institute.

1976 Dr. Bath cofounded the American Institute for the Prevention of Blindness, which helps prevent blindness worldwide.

1981 She started developing an invention that would use lasers to remove cataracts.

1988 Dr. Bath received her first patent. She was the first African American female doctor to receive a medical patent.

1994 Dr. Bath traveled the world, teaching other doctors how to perform KPRO (keratoprosthesis) eye surgery. In Tunisia, inside an airplane, she operated on two patients who had been blind for decades. When Dr. Bath peeled away their bandages, her patients gasped—they could finally see the faces of their children!

2009 Dr. Bath was recognized by President Obama for her work with the blind.

2019 This amazing doctor, inventor, and teacher passed away on May 30, 2019.

NOTE FROM THE AUTHOR

I discovered Dr. Patricia Bath when I was researching "female firsts" for a project. My mother had been recently diagnosed with cataracts, so I was especially interested to learn about the woman who invented the laser probe used to remove cataracts. As a child I, too, wanted to be a doctor when I grew up. In fact, my project for the elementary school science fair focused on eyes, complete with a dissected cow eyeball.

Dr. Bath and I discussed her life over a series of telephone interviews. I feel that this inspiring woman has been overlooked for too long, and I hope this book is a fitting tribute to her incredible life.

Many thanks to Leslie J. Pollard, BSMT, LEOT, CMLSO, Laser Education Specialist, and Qing Qing Wang, Electrical Engineering PhD, Development Engineer, for lending their expertise.

MORE ABOUT DR. PATRICIA BATH

Patricia Bath was born on November 4, 1942, in Harlem, New York City. Some may have considered the Bath family impoverished, but Patricia felt rich! Her mother, Gladys, took care of the family. Big brother taught her how to read. Her father, Rupert, was an immigrant from Trinidad who spoke his mind and didn't let racism keep him down. At one time, he worked in the New York City subway system as the first black motorman. He fought against the discrimination of black workers and strove to protect their rights. Patricia learned a lifelong lesson from her father—to stand up for what she believed in.

When Patricia applied to college, the interviewer told her that an education was a waste for women. At the time, many women worked as secretaries, nurses, and sales clerks. Some went to college to find a husband. But Patricia was determined to get an education. She enrolled at Hunter College, where she earned her undergraduate degree.

America was changing. African Americans struggled for equal rights. Patricia met Dr. Martin Luther King, Jr., at a rally in 1964; his words vibrated through her body. He wanted equality for *all* people. He thought that nobody should go without food or medical care. Patricia was inspired by Dr. King. "I want to help!" She volunteered for the Poor People's Campaign that Dr. King had envisioned before he was assassinated.

As an intern at Harlem Hospital, Dr. Bath discovered that blindness was twice as common in black patients compared to white patients. She came up with a new idea she called *community ophthalmology*. It offered eye care and blindness prevention to underserved communities.

Dr. Bath lived her lifelong goal of helping the blind. Countless people have benefitted from her Laserphaco Probe.